THE ART *of* WENDY FROUD

THE ART *of* WENDY FROUD

IMAGINOSIS
LOS ANGELES

With thanks to:

Stephanie Lostimolo, Jake Lebovic, and especially Robert Gould for putting this book together so beautifully and to Brian Froud for his fantastic photography. Thank you to Richard Taylor and to all of the people who have supported my work over the years, especially Angi Sullins, Neil Zuckerman, Thomas Boland and Sideshow Collectables.

Cover Design: Brian Froud
Graphic Design: Stephanie Lostimolo, Jake Lebovic
Art Direction: Robert Gould
Editing: Ari Berk

Library of Congress Cataloging-in-Publication Data has been applied for.
ISBN: 0-9779956-0-7

Printed in China by Regent Publishing Services Limited.
10 9 8 7 6 5 4 3 2 1

An IMAGINOSIS Book.

Please visit the Official World of Froud website:
WorldofFroud.com.

IMAGINOSIS
A TRANSMEDIA ARTS COMPANY
4195 Crisp Canyon
Sherman Oaks, CA
91403
Imaginosis.com

To Peggy and Walter Midener, my mother and father.

With profound thanks and gratitude to:
Brian, Robert, Ari, Toby, Todd and Guy,
the occasionally lost boys who, with their love
and belief in me, built the Wendy House.

FOREWORD

Deep in the Devon countryside, Tania and I were on a journey that would deliver us from everyday reality into a place of enchantment and fantasy. Threading our way between high hedgerows and carefully weaving down tight, meandering roads in our car, we followed the path of our map. Finally turning into a narrow, shaded lane beneath a great oak tree, we found ourselves in the world of the Frouds.

We were both greatly privileged to be able to go and spend a few hours in the company of Wendy, Brian and Toby Froud, enjoying, not only their hospitality, but also experiencing the magic and artistic beauty of a very special family. It was some years ago now, but the friendship that we found and the magic we experienced that day have remained with us ever since.

In Wendy's studio and home, we found ourselves immersed in a magical place where her art had formed its own reality. With childlike wonder, we were transported into the realm of her imagination, watched and surrounded by many tiny pairs of pixie eyes.

The intricacy of the costuming, delicate sculptural finesse of her faces, exquisite miniature props, and the enchanted environments of Wendy's creations were not only uplifting to view, but seemed imbued with otherworldly spirits that could whisk one away on a whimsical journey out beyond the edge of the garden or across the sun — dappled brook. Her figures had an incredible delicacy, yet each one also had eyes that sparkled with a life and vitality breathed into their bodies by Wendy herself.

Though our time in Devon was short, Tania and I were fortunate enough to bring home some of Wendy's creatures. These little goblins now sit upon our bedside mantelpiece, watching over us through the night – Froudian guardians that conjure up our dreams, and, I suspect, perpetrate many a sneaky mischief in our house while we sleep.

Wendy's art has touched many of us over the years. Her characters and environments let us into a world that is less troubled than our own, filled with gentle beauty, mysticism, and spirituality. One can escape with them to a simpler place where our childhood dreams still dwell.

It is inspirational to witness each new piece that Wendy creates, unabashed in its celebration of the pure fantasy of her imagination, inspired by the folklore of the past and the quiet beauty of her home.

And now the wonders that we witnessed firsthand have been captured in this incredible book, a body of work that is testament to a rich tapestry of lore and beauty that Wendy has woven of fantasy, faeries, goblins and all things mystical and delightful.

Wendy is a unique artist who weaves spirit and vitality into the characters that spring from her fingers and live in her heart. It is an honour for me to write this Foreword for her book, an incredible compilation of images by one of Britain's most unique and accomplished fantasy artists, and I am touched and thrilled to have been asked.

To you, Wendy, we all say, "thank you." We thank you for being the keeper of our childhood dreams and, through your art, connecting us with that innocence that we had so long thought lost and gone.

Richard Taylor
Weta Workshop
March 2006

INTRODUCTION

What is a doll? Is it just something that a child, especially a girl-child, plays with? Is it an evocation of a past age, an embodiment of innocence that we as adults like to believe in? Or is it something we create to explore fantasies and dreams? Is it a channel for communication between a person and other worlds, a conduit between the real world and the world of the imagination? A vehicle for soul, a house for spirit? I hope so. For me a doll is all of these things. It always has been.

One of my earliest memories is visiting my uncle's toy factory in Sao Paulo, Brazil, when I was about two years old. I remember shelf upon shelf of toys in the showroom, but most of all I remember a conveyer belt of seemingly endless doll heads moving past me as I watched. I've found that mass-produced toys and dolls have bothered me ever since and I still look carefully at each individual toy, certain that I'll be able to spot the one with the most personality. The need for expressing personality when creating

a character, whether it be human or creature, has always been central to my work.

I was always encouraged to make things by my artist parents. Anything I could imagine, I was told, I could make real in some form. I could draw or paint it, I could write about it, I could sculpt it in clay, I could make it come to life by turning it into a doll – a moving, interactive object that could lead me into realms of the imagination and accompany me on the journey, always faithful, always ready to lead me back home at the end of the adventure. And so I did. I began my doll-making career at the age of about five and have continued to make dolls and figures, fetishes and sculptures, puppets and models, all my life. It is such an integral part of me that I can't imagine not doing it.

I began by making dolls from old socks, bits of felt, yarn, pipe cleaners, and wooden balls. They may not have looked like anything to an adult, but to me they were just what

I needed to expand my play world into the fantasy realms I longed to be a part of. My mother enriched and encouraged this by reading to me every night. That was always a magical time before bed because she enjoyed the stories as much as I did. Together we explored Narnia, Middle Earth, Oz, the many realms of Faery, and the English countryside, woodland, and riverbank, in the company of children, elves, animals, centaurs, faeries, Hobbits, dragons, a sand fairy, and a phoenix. Detroit couldn't hold a candle to the worlds we explored.

I went to Interlochen Arts Academy for high school, becoming a drama major after a short and disastrous attempt at playing the viola. I was much more suited to a life of make-believe. In my spare time I still made toys and dolls as presents for people and for myself as well, using old fur coats and whatever I could lay my hands on, fabric-wise. I then attended CCS (Center For Creative Studies – College of Art and Design) in Detroit. My parents both worked there, my mother teaching painting and my father as first the head of the sculpture department and then president of the school. I had been involved with the school since I was born and really thought of it as an extension of family life. I didn't feel that I could take either painting or sculpture since my parents were so much a part of those fields, so I became a fabric design major, studying ceramics and jewelry as well. This suited me perfectly since I could apply the things I learned in these disciplines to my doll making. I'm sure that my long-suffering instructors didn't quite know what to make of my insistence on turning every project into something doll – fantasy – related, but as long as I learned the skills being taught, they just let me get on with it. I loved it and squirreled away all of the information I acquired for later use.

After graduating, I moved with a group of friends to New York to seek fame and fortune, or at least a job as a waitress. Instead, I was offered a job with the Muppets. Michael Frith, the art director of the Muppets, came to a studio exhibition of my work in the loft that my best friend Guy and I shared. Michael bought one of my puppets as a Christmas gift for Jim Henson, and early in January he called to ask me if I would like to come to the workshop for an interview with Jim about a new project they were planning. Being able to do the thing I loved more than anything, and perhaps even get paid for it, was more than I had dared hope for when I graduated from Art College.

I spent the next eight years first in New York and then in London as part of an amazing team of artists and craftspeople led by the master magician Jim Henson, creating magic that would

9

touch and inspire people around the world. *The Muppet Show, The Dark Crystal, The Empire Strikes Back,* and *Labyrinth* were all projects that I was involved with as a sculptor and puppet builder. Of course, one of the most wonderful things was meeting, working with and marrying Brian Froud. Together we worked on many challenging and innovative characters, but creating our son Toby was our finest achievement.

After *Labyrinth* ended, we moved as a family back down to Dartmoor in Devon. Brian began painting and drawing again for books he was working on and I became a full-time mother. This was not always easy since Toby and I are both extremely strong-willed. Brian often had to separate us and send us to our rooms after a particularly ferocious argument over what we should build with Lego, Toby tending towards spaceships and me preferring sphinxes. We never could agree.

Since I was now at home, I began once again to make dolls and puppets, which I gave to friends or sold locally. I began using Brian's sketchbooks as references and applying the skills I learned from my years as a sculptor and puppet builder to my doll making. I enjoyed just being at home and in our village, doing what I loved but not thinking about reaching a wider audience. Then about twelve years ago my friend Guy met Thomas Boland, the premier doll artist agent in the U.S., and told me that I must get in contact with him. It was time to go out into the wider world again. I met Tom, and for

years he and the Thomas Boland Company very successfully represented me at doll and toy shows around the U.S. and I found that I loved the contact with buyers and the public. It was wonderful to get a response from people who seemed to be drawn to what I made. At this time I also met Neil Zuckerman, owner of the CFM gallery in New York, and took part in *The Doll As Art,* a series of exhibitions he mounted along with many of the best and most innovative doll artists working at the time. These exhibitions gave us exposure as artists in our own right as well as doll makers. To be taken seriously as an artist and craftsperson is important, and Neil made sure that it happened.

Over the years Brian and I have become even more of a team, creating "The World Of Froud" with our friend and business partner, Robert Gould. Robert continues to encourage us (sometimes with a big stick) to go out into the world and meet the people we touch through our work. Under the *World of Froud* banner I have published three books with my friend, the author Terri Windling, using photos of my pieces to illustrate the stories she wrote for the characters. I've also contributed to the book *Goblins!* by Brian Froud and Ari Berk, and Brian and I continue to develop projects together.

People often ask me how I make what I make and where my influences come from. I've been inspired, as I said, by the myths, fairy tales, and novels, I read and heard as a child and student. Other influences include Brian's work, Robert Holdstock's *Mythago Wood* novels and *Little, Big* by John Crowley, which made a great impression on me as an adult. One influence that I find most enduring is *The Fairy Tale Book,* a Golden Press book

illustrated by Adrienne Segur. I grew up with this large book, spending hours poring over the intricate illustrations of bejeweled cats, deer-headed men, faeries, princesses, and talking beasts. I could lose myself in them, and the wistful faces and beautiful clothing still remain a part of my own world. I have since found that this particular book has also influenced many (and I really do mean many) other fantasy artists, doll artists and writers. I have also always loved the work of the Pre-Raphaelite artists, again not only for their subject matter, but for the sumptuous costumes, otherworldly expressions and flowing red hair.

Greek mythology has played an important part in informing my imagery and personal myth world. I love the interaction of men and gods and the havoc it usually creates, which is also one of the most enticing aspects of the interaction between the world of humans and Faerie. Although I love to create dolls and figures that will make people smile, I also like them to have a quality of mystery, of the unknowable about them, something that makes them feel not altogether safe or comfortable.

How do I physically make what I make? I start by making an armature out of wire. I sculpt the head, hands, and feet, or any parts of the figure that will be seen without clothing onto the wire armature in FIMO polymer clay that I mix up to my own specification from various colors and textures. After baking this, I usually use small pieces of wood doweling to make "bones" which I tape and glue to the wire so that the piece can only bend at the joints. I

then cover that with polyester fiberfill and sew a stretchy "skin" of fabric over that to make a body that I can sew clothes to. I paint the face and exposed skin with acrylic paint, in thin washes or applied like makeup with sponges. I don't use glass eyes. I prefer to sculpt them directly into the face and paint them, finishing them with a spot of clear varnish. I use many different types of hair, from human to Persian lamb — what ever looks best on an individual piece — gluing it in place a few hairs at a time.

When I go out hunting for fabrics, I spend a great deal of time thinking about scale and weight and what will look natural on something so much smaller than a human. I have found that silks in all forms are the very best fabrics to use. They drape beautifully whether they are the finest chiffons or the roughest unspun silk weave, and works in all scales, so I can use it for tiny figures as well as very large pieces. You can age a piece of silk to look like anything from a queen's robe to a beggar's rags and it will still have an authentic feel about it.

I have a magpie-like need to collect things, especially beautiful or interesting fabrics and soft leather pieces, beads and trimmings. My studio cupboards are overflowing with the spoils of my treasure hunting. I like to decide what a figure will wear after I have finished the body construction. I have found many times in the past that if I decide on what the finished piece will look like too early on in the process, it inevitably changes along the way and turns into something completely different. Women who start out as dazzling blondes end up as black-

haired vixens. If they start out as princesses they end up as woodland elven queens. Sometimes I feel that I have no real control over what they will be. After I get them to a certain point they seem to take over and decide for themselves what their future will be. As I write this, I can see that it sounds crazy, but then I never said I was particularly sane.

That's it, I suppose: how I came to do what I do and how I do it. I like to think of myself and my work as part of a continuous lineage of makers and objects stretching back to the first cave people who made little figures of ivory, wood and clay. Dolls have been with us in the form of playthings, fetishes or magical objects since we began to create inner worlds to help explain our everyday existence, or to help us rise above the ordinary in our lives. They are an intrinsic part of what we as human beings are, illuminating our psyches, becoming our companions on our inner adventures and sharing in our spiritual quests for the Otherworld. Long may they continue to be with us, and I thank the universe for letting me be a part of that lineage.

Wendy Froud

Romantica

I love the idea of creating or implying relation-
ships in the pieces I make, either by placing two
or more figures together or by using gesture,
expression, or costume to suggest that a relationship might exist between the figure I've sculpted
and some other unseen character known only
to the doll. The back-story, the mystery, the
romance of a piece is very appealing to me.
I know that each figure has a story to tell.
I might not always be sure of what it is, but
more often than not the piece itself will reveal
its story to me as I work on it.

Red hair is my favorite hair color for dolls.
I have to stop myself from giving them all red
hair. I think perhaps my fixation on red hair
came from my love of Pre-Raphaelite paintings.
Red was the preferred color for hair in the
paintings that influenced me the most or the ones
that I identified with most strongly. Red-haired

people are set apart; they are slightly of the
Otherworld. I suppose since my family back-
ground is Celtic, at least on my mother's side,
red hair is naturally a part of my history.

Color and texture are so important when
choosing how to dress a piece. If I'm stuck
for ideas of what to make, sometimes I'll lay
out pieces of fabric just picked at random
and see what they suggest to me. They often
will spark off an idea that ends up having
nothing to do with the fabrics I chose but,
nonetheless, they will have been the inspiration
for it.

One of the best things about working in
a relatively small scale is that I can use very
expensive materials because I use such small
amounts. Gem stones, gold leaf, hand-embroidered
fabrics, fine silk velvets, and antique beading
are my favorite indulgences.

Being a mother has been an amazing experience. In a way, I feel as though I've been a mother to every doll I've made, and collaborating with Brian once again to produce our son, Toby, was certainly our crowning achievement. When Toby was little, before he could object, I made all sorts of costumes for him, dressing him up like a bunny, a teddy bear, a jester, an elf. He must have enjoyed it as much as Brian and I did because as soon as he could talk, he demanded costumes – Ninja Turtles, Spiderman, monsters, anything he could think of. His

experience as the baby in *Labyrinth* and his early life among puppets, film sets, and adults who do strange and interesting things for a living gave him the confidence to stride through situations that terrify me. I have to remind myself constantly that he's perfectly capable of looking after himself. Of course, being his mother and "Wendy" as well, I do always make sure that his shadow is sewn on tightly before I let him go out into the world-at-large. It's been wonderful to see him grow up to be not only an extremely competent and sensitive

sculptor but also a performer who can bring any character to life, be it a dancing bear, a stilted dragon, a satyr, or a buxom Faery Godmother on bouncing stilts — all costumes that I've recently made for him. I think that working and playing together have kept Brian and me young as Toby has grown up. In many ways, we all meet as equals now, and the ability to share ideas, working methods, and projects has enriched all of our lives.

I've said before that relationship and story are crucial to my creative process. This piece is a good example of a story implied but not directly depicted. The girl, in medieval dress, is holding a unicorn's horn and a golden bridle. This suggests that she is a virgin in some sort of relationship with a unicorn. Has something just happened or is something about to happen? Has she just captured, bridled and then killed a unicorn? Has she taken the horn and bridle as trophies, or is she keeping the unicorn enthralled while the huntsmen surround it for the kill? Perhaps she isn't going to do either. She may be stealing the bridle away and hiding the ceremonial horn so that the unicorn will be safe. I don't know. Only she knows what's going on, but so far she has not felt obliged to tell me.

I hope that by experiencing my work, people will be encouraged to explore their own personal fantasy world — that they will be able to use my images as signposts and gateways into worlds that they may have visited as children but forgotten about as adults. Imagination is so important. Being a part of something that sparks imagination in others is one of the things that makes what I do the most worthwhile to me.

I love the mysterious nature of working on something that has an unforeseen conclusion. I can hardly ever visualize a finished piece in detail and have it come out as I saw it in my mind. There are too many factors involved, from the first lump of clay to the last stitch in the fabric, to be able to know what the final piece will look like. Or perhaps I really mean *feel* like. A figure can have a totally different feel to it than what I visualized, even when it physically ends up looking like what I intended to make in the first place.

I have often had people write to me or come up to me rather sheepishly and say that they just know that the doll of mine they have moves around at night. They're never upset by it; rather, they seem to be intrigued, but they come to me expecting answers to this phenomenon and I'm afraid I can't tell them anything. I don't know if they move or not. I do know that they have a lot of energy in them. Whatever that energy is, I can always reassure people that it isn't harmful. I never put angry energy into a piece. I never sculpt when I'm personally angry — sad, yes, melancholy or pensive, certainly, but never angry.

Fantastica

Alice In Wonderland and Through the Looking Glass are two of the most important books that I grew up with. The images in them have stayed with me and I've often sculpted Alice and the other characters in those stories. Elements of the illustrations I was especially fond of when I was little continue to turn up. Striped stockings, top hats, elaborate and dishevelled dresses, and odd old ladies are all favorite images. Fairy tales and children's stories are an endless source of inspiration. Baba Yaga and her house on chicken legs still fascinate me. It is one of the pieces I'm planning to make in the near future. Cinderella, any sleeping princess, and fairy godmothers are all rich images with endless variations. I find it interesting that we tend to think of children's stories as simple, cheerful tales but in reality they are incredibly complex stories that are hardly ever cheerful. Happy endings are never as happy as you think they'll be and even the heroes aren't always very pleasant. Fairy tales are like dolls themselves, not considered something of interest to adults until you look at them individually and realize how sophisticated they can be.

Angelica

The idea of angelic beings looking out for us is very comforting. While sculpting an angel it's easy to feel the shelter of their wings and a protective and inspiring presence hovering close. I've made many angel figures. I think I first started making them when I was at art school. Maybe it's the anatomy — the idea of human forms with enormous feathered wings growing out of their backs — that is so intriguing. When you think about it, they shouldn't have arms but of course they do. I find Lucifer as a fallen angel especially interesting; the light-bringer, the most beautiful angel of them all, the eternal exile. Very romantic, really, in a dark, gothic sort of way!

An important element of my working regime is music. I always have music playing while I work. If I'm writing I need complete silence; otherwise, I can't hear the words as they form in my head and I write them down; but when I sculpt or costume I need music. I love sculpting to Mozart and Bach: Mozart when I'm trying to get the feel of a character, trying to figure out who it wants to be as I'm sculpting, and Bach when I need a clear run at just getting down to concentrating on things like hands and feet. Music helps to take me beyond myself, beyond the task at hand. I don't see in pictures when I listen to music

but it does free me to think about things that I associate with what I'm hearing. Sometimes an image will float up to the surface, revealing something I hadn't thought about in years. Music seems to be a key to the strange memory rooms we all have in our minds, that open when we hear a certain sound or sequence of notes or lyrics. The images that appear always turn out to be relevant to what I'm working on in some way, although it isn't always clear at the time what the music wants me to see.

While sculpting I often listen to June Tabor, the amazing British folk singer. Her songs move me to tears every time I hear them but there's something about her voice and the instrumental backing she uses that transport me to a place where I can put that emotion into the face I'm sculpting. I suppose that's one of the reasons that so many of my dolls have such pensive looks on their faces. They, along with me, have heard the voice of love lost, friends betrayed, soldiers dying on the battlefield, the poignancy of a miner's life and all of the experiences that June puts into her music.

Inspiration is a sacred gift. Throughout my career, inspiration has come from wonderous sources. From the moment I walked in to the interview with Jim Henson to work on *Dark Crystal*, I knew that he was an incredibly special

individual. That might sound a bit obvious, but I really mean that Jim was special on a world level and the energy that surrounded him made that quite clear from the beginning. He nurtured creativity in all of the people that worked for and with him. As individuals we were always made to feel that we had something important to bring to the project as a whole. At the same time, Jim had very strong views about what he wanted or didn't want. When I sculpted the Gelflings, Jen and Kira, Jim would come by my desk and look at them and say something like "That's not quite it yet. I'll know it when I see it." This could be very frustrating, especially if Brian had just come by before Jim and said "Yes, I think that's what I'm looking for," or if Frank Oz or Gary Kurtz had just done the same thing, each with a different opinion. I learned to sculpt very fast and change the look of a character in a few minutes. Fun, frustration, hard, hard work, and a huge sense of accomplishment were what came from working with Jim, as well as a life-long friendship that I continue to value as one of the most precious things in my life.

In the first few days after 9/11 I, like most of the people around me, felt helpless and at a loss as to what I could personally do to respond to an act that changed our concept of the world as we know it. I have no natural instinct for revenge and I couldn't imagine responding in an aggressive or angry way. Not that I wasn't angry and appalled, but I couldn't imagine creating something from that anger. The image that kept coming into my mind was that of an angelic figure who was full of compassion – not blame, not revenge, but a caring for everyone affected by the bombing no matter who or where they were. I wanted to make something that would evoke a sense of peace and hope. I've used this image many times since I first made it, and it recently spent a week on the altar of our village church during Harvest Festival.

Faerieana

I was named for the Wendy in *Peter Pan*. I think that has always colored my view of life. I was devastated when I realized that I was too old to go to Neverland and that Peter wasn't going to come for me. Then, much later, when I was really grown up, I realized that I could create my own Neverland by doing what I do and sharing it with the world at large. That's the good thing about growing up: it allows you to realize your dreams.

From a very early age, when my mother began to read books to me, she read stories that were set mainly in other worlds but that inevitably began and ended in England. This was usually a comfortable Victorian or at least pre-nineteen fifties England with long summers, ginger beer and an adventure around every corner. When I finally came to visit England for the first time, it still had many of those qualities I so longed to experience from those childhood books. It still has. I live on Dartmoor, a wild and in some ways austere part of southwest England. We are surrounded by rolling hills, topped by huge granite outcroppings called *tors*. They rise like prehistoric cathedrals above the small valleys filled with stunted oak trees, moss – covered boulders, and sparkling streams. The legends that are attached to them are full of faeries, pixies and supernatural beings of all kinds, from spectral black dogs to ghostly highwaymen. Our house – nestled in one of these valleys – is dated as late medieval but its

foundations are much older than that. To a girl from Detroit, this is an astonishingly ancient place to live, and yet I feel more at home here than I have ever felt anywhere else. Many people in this area feel that the veil between the worlds is especially thin in our part of the country and I have to agree. Perhaps that's why creating creatures and otherworldly people comes easily to me here. Maybe they just wander into my psyche from the Otherworld — the world of Faerie — as easily as I walk from one room to another.

For me, the real difference between the world of Faerie and the larger world of myth is that Faerie is so immediate, so intimate. Faerie is close by us all the time, far closer feeling than the epic landscapes of some of the world's myths. Faerie exists in parallel to our world. Occasionally, we can touch it, see it, and experience it when the division between the two worlds is thin enough. The nature of Faerie is a very personal thing. Now, everyone has their own idea of what it is, what it looks and feels like. Brian and I try to show people what our experience of Faerie is by the art we produce. Often people will say that the work looks "real" to them. They don't just mean that it looks lifelike but that it looks like how they experience Faerie as well. We tap into something that can be a universal experience. These characters that Brian and I produce are just as valid, just as "real" in Japan and Australia, France, Germany, and Italy as they are in England and America.

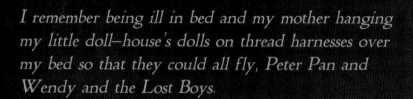

I remember being ill in bed and my mother hanging
my little doll–house's dolls on thread harnesses over
my bed so that they could all fly, Peter Pan and
Wendy and the Lost Boys.

In my fantasies, all my dolls could fly.
All of them were magic.

Often when I work, especially when I'm at the sculpting stage at the beginning of a piece, I find that I have no recollection of time spent, no sense that time has passed. I can sit down to work at nine in the morning and the next time I look at the clock, it's one o'clock and time to stop for lunch. I have a sculpted head in my hands that has already developed a personality and I'm not quite sure how it got there. I tend to think about things that have absolutely no bearing on what I'm sculpting, like what's going to happen next in the soap opera I watch in the evenings (*East Enders* has always been a favorite). How mundane is that! I've solved the problems in the lives of more fictional characters than I care to think about. But maybe, just maybe, it's all part of the same process. Making, creating, fixing. That's what I do with my hands, so why wouldn't I try to do it in my imagination as well?

I was introduced to Brian's work by Jim Henson on the day I was hired to work on a new project called *The Dark Crystal*. Jim showed me books of Brian's art called *The Land Of Froud* and *Once Upon A Time*, saying that this was the person who would be designing the film. We in the workshop were to bring his drawings and paintings to three-dimensional life. I had never before seen fantasy painting and illustration that touched me as Brian's did. I grew up loving Arthur Rackham's illustrations, but these had a life and an immediacy to them that went far beyond illustration. It was as though Brian had reached into the world of Faerie and brought out creatures that no one had ever thought of before, but once seen were as familiar (albeit strangely) as the neighbor's cat. I found it very easy to look at the sketches and then sculpt them in three dimensions. They were waiting to be released from the page so that they could inhabit this world as fully and immediately as their own. Ours is a marriage of heart and art. It has remained one of my greatest pleasures to sculpt from Brian's designs and see these creatures take form in front of us in all of their mischievous glory.

Occasionally when I've finished a piece, especially when it's one that I've taken from a sketch by Brian, I just know that we'll have trouble in the house until it settles in and decides to behave. When I made Gargle for the *Goblins!* book (not shown in this book – *much* too dangerous), we had no end of household disasters in the following days – a small flood, lights exploding, power cuts, spills and breakages. Brian finally had to take Gargle in to his studio and keep him out of sight until he changed his ways.

Gargle is now very well-behaved and a model goblin. Sometimes the creatures just have a wild look in their eyes after I put the finishing touches on them and then we know that we must tread gently. I try not to send pieces off to people until they're house-trained but accidents do happen as the workshop of Sideshow Collectables can attest to. While they were molding and casting pixies for me the pixies created havoc and finally had to be soothed with pieces of chocolate left near them at night.

Gothica

I love the dark and modern side of Faerie.
The idea that Faerie is just as present, just as
tangible, in an inner city is intriguing and
important because it makes the old stories
relevant to the modern world. It may be because
I grew up in Detroit and spent my childhood
not only making up worlds but having an equal
amount of fun playing in alleyways that makes
it easy for me to picture the world of Faerie
leaking out from behind trash cans and reflecting
in oily puddles of gasoline. I have a need to
people that world with my dolls. Besides, it's fun
to make things that are a bit darker sometimes.
"Goth" is a great expression of dark fantasy,
the clothes and hair add a bit of faery glamour
and the dangerous city world of Faerie begins
to come alive. Many of my favorite authors
have written brilliant stories about cities where
humans and faeries collide and coexist and I
do have to admit that I'm a *Buffy The Vampire
Slayer* fan as well!

   I'm a compulsive reader. If I have an
addiction, reading is it. I feel very uneasy if
I don't have a book lined up to start as soon
as I finish the one I'm reading at the moment.
I've often wondered why reading is so important
to me, and I should qualify that by saying that
it's fiction that is most important of all. I do
read factual books but fiction is my love. Not
necessarily fantasy fiction either. I love any kind
of character study and I apply my reading to
the characters I make. I am what I would call a
visual reader. I see pictures the whole time I'm
reading so it's really like one, long movie, art
directed by myself, every time I pick up a book.
I often "see" characters that I know I will end up

sculpting or become involved in situations within a novel that I can then transfer to my characters. Written descriptions of people and places, emotions and situations, are endlessly stimulating to my own creativity.

People often ask me how I feel about selling my dolls, how I feel about sending them away. It's difficult. Often, I make dolls specifically to sell or for someone in particular. Those are easier to send off because I've woven that intent into them as I worked on them, but occasionally I've found that when I've completed a doll for a specific purpose it just doesn't want to leave. There is something about it that makes keeping it with me important, at least for a while. It usually turns out that the piece becomes central to something we're working on and, for obvious reasons soon made apparent, needed to stay with us. I do send each one off with the intention that it will help whoever it is going to in some way. I think of my dolls as messengers bringing healing to their new owners. If I resented selling them or sending them off, it would defeat the purpose of making them.

Methusa

My parents introduced me to ancient art at a
very early age. Greek culture, both mythic and
historical, held a great fascination for my parents
and they passed that interest and love on to me.
When I was nine we went to Europe for the
summer and spent a month in Greece, based in
Athens and touring around the ancient sites on
the mainland and the islands. My mother and

I read Greek myths and *The Ilia*
Odyssey (it must have been a chi
version) to prepare for the trip. M
mother were both very interested i
and our dinner discussions center
ancient temples, statues and gods ar
Where they came from – how they
was something that we investigated

was always made to feel that my observations were valuable. There is mystery and magic in old places that have been occupied by humans for thousands of years. The fact that we don't know everything – and in some cases very little – about those ancient cultures makes them very enticing. To be able to walk where a Greek hero died or a god was born is a magical thing. I've always felt a need to somehow capture some of that magic in figures when I make centaurs, fauns, gods and goddesses. It's my way of tangibly connecting with a world that more readily accepts creatures that our own modern culture often dismisses as mere fantasy. If the ancient Greeks carved huge friezes depicting a battle between centaurs and men or the birth of the goddess Aphrodite then that's good enough for me! I'm a believer.

Half animal, half human: the Greeks had many such combinations in their pantheon of demigods and monsters. They were all beings that could and did communicate with humans, except the minotaur — that poor beast who had the head of a bull and the body of a man — all he did was eat them. Sphinxes, centaurs, faun and satyrs — the great god Pan himself — they were dangerous, but still they were rational. Face to face with a sphinx, you had a fighting chance to come out of it alive if you kept your wits about you, but facing the minotaur, that was a different thing entirely. Of course, in the end, even the minotaur met his match. Theseus killed the beast and escaped with the king's daughter, not that it did him much good. Heroes as well as monsters often have unfulfilled lives. I love these combinations and the challenge of creating something believable but sympathetic. Again, it's the relationship, in this case between two halves of the same creature, that I find fascinating.

The green man is such an ancient image. It is seen now mostly in early Christian churches, usually hidden away high in the roof bosses, a symbol of wild nature looking down into the body of the church itself. As an image, it has appealed to me since I first encountered it when I moved to Devon, though I never felt the need to make it, to explore the energy behind the image, until I read the *Mythago Wood* series of books by Robert Holdstock. His writing brought the green man and, indeed, the green woman startlingly to life for me, and it was Holdstock's use of mask imagery that immediately sent me into my studio to create these beings for myself. They seem to have a wild energy about them that I never intentionally put there. Perhaps it is just inherent in that image. For some reason, they seem to drive cats crazy. I've made quite a few versions of the green man and they are never safe from attack when cats are near. They are unsettling, even to me. Of all the pieces I've created the green man masks are the least domesticated. They are powerful but unpredictable icons, bringing the wild magic into our world.

FAERY TALES

When I was young and foolish
and a princess or a milkmaid
or a goosegirl,
I wished for things and got them,
good and bad, gold and toads,
for better or worse,
for happily ever after,
or not.

I slept and woke,
sang amongst the ashes or was mute,
lived in the tower, the castle,
the cottage,
married my prince, my king,
my woodcutter,
lived happily ever after,
my days measured by the
turn of a season, the phase of a moon
and in the end, I died
and in my place, a daughter or a son
or something else entirely
wished, as I had done.

But now, here is the part I like,
where I become the one
to grant those wishes as I please
and I do.
Snakes and lizards, toads.
diamonds, pearls and gold.
a poison apple, gingerbread,
a pumpkin coach, a gilded dress.
Tools of my trade, my teaching aids.
My gifts, my curses.
Prince to frog, frog to prince,
iron shoes and feet that dance
and dance and dance
and I like it both ways,
like to bless them
and eat them.
Diamonds and blood,
bones and gold.
It's all happily ever after to me.

— *Wendy Froud*